Weeping Before an Emp[ty Tomb] [is a] book in its own right [...] titled *Soul Survivor Life.*

The aim of the series is to explain the basics of Christianity and Christian living in down-to-earth, jargon-free language. The four books follow the pattern of life: birth, adolescence, mid-life crisis and death. The first, *Walking with a Stranger*, explores what it really means to become a Christian, who God is and how we can build a personal relationship with him. *My First Trousers* looks at the challenges and rewards facing us when we start going deeper with Jesus. The Christian life is not easy, however, and *Weeping Before an Empty Tomb* asks how we cope when the going gets tough. The final book, *Afterlife*, is about facing the future, in particular death, heaven and eternity.

Mike Pilavachi is the founder of Soul Survivor and pastor of Soul Survivor, Watford. Craig Borlase is a free-lance writer. They have previously written two other books together, *Live the Life* and *For the Audience of One* (both Hodder Christian Books).

Weeping Before an Empty Tomb

Struggling with God

Mike Pilavachi with Craig Borlase

Hodder & Stoughton
LONDON SYDNEY AUCKLAND

Copyright © Mike Pilavachi and Craig Borlase 2000

First published in Great Britain in 2000

The right of Mike Pilavachi and Craig Borlase to be identified as the
Authors of the Work has been asserted by them in accordance with
the Copyright, Designs and Patents Act 1988.

10 9 8 7 6 5 4 3 2 1

British Library Cataloguing in Publication Data
A record for this book is available from the British Library

ISBN 0 340 73536 8

Typeset by Avon Dataset Ltd, Bidford-on-Avon, Warks

Printed and bound in Great Britain by
Clays Ltd, St Ives plc

Hodder & Stoughton Ltd
A Division of Hodder Headline
338 Euston Road
London NW1 3BH

To Ken and Jeannie Morgan.
Thank you for your faithful 'partnership in the gospel'
for all these years. May there be many more to come.

Contents

Acknowledgements

I would like to thank my friends at Soul Survivor who, when I felt like I was sinking, jumped in to save the drowning man. To Liz, who not only read the manuscript and made her usual wise comments but also cancelled my appointments on a couple of days and did not tell me until the night before. To Martyn Layzell, Carole Japtha and Neil Pearce, for their helpful suggestions and comments. To Jonathan Stevens, for his servant heart, enthusiasm and efficiency. To J. John, who has once again proved an invaluable honorary research assistant. There has not yet been an occasion when I have popped round to the Johns for coffee and not left with bags full of books, pamphlets and transcripts of past J. John sermons to help me on my way. To Matt and Beth Redman, the drama of whose lives keeps me entertained and anxious in equal measure. Let's hope the little one gets to lead a quieter life. Some hope!

To Ben Morrison, 'my soultimer', who has been a fantastic research assistant. To David Moloney, our editor at Hodder – thanks for your patience and continual flexibility, especially when it came to the deadlines. Last but by no means least, to Craig Borlase, whose friendship is a joy to me and whose writing skills never cease to amaze me. Thank you, little ones!

1

Weeping Before an Empty Tomb

Mary's Story

Picture me at the age of sixteen; lithe, witty, intelligent and charming, wearing the very latest in three-tone brown tank tops and riddled with all the confusion of a young man who had just discovered that girls were nice but almost impossible to talk to. It was at this age that I wrote painful poetry and tried to work out the meaning of life in Harrow. It was also at this age that my dad made me the best promise ever.

It was 1974 and my dad had, for some reason that I still have trouble working out, gone out one day and bought a brand-new car. Looking out of my bedroom window I was amazed to see him cruise around the corner in a limited edition, black, three-door Fiat Cinquecento. I was amazed, proud and scared witless (my first thought being that my dad had become a member of the local Greek Mafia). I soon calmed down though and allowed my natural boyish fascination with all things mechanical/ dangerous to take over. I cooed, wowed and dribbled over it with such intensity that I hardly noticed that my dad was trying to talk to me.

'Mike, this is for you. As soon as you're seventeen and have passed your test you can have it.'

Pretty soon I was hyperventilating with excitement. This was without doubt the best present I had ever been given and the euphoria stayed around for days. I thought about it, dreamt about it and told all my friends, ex-friends and total strangers all about My New Car. I was – to put it mildly – on a buzz.

Not everyone believed me, which was a shame but perhaps not all that surprising. What did surprise me, though, was the fact that a few months after that wonderful day, my dad started using *my car*. He said that it was just because his had broken down, and at first he insisted that his borrowing changed nothing. The months went by, his car went to the scrapheap and my old man settled back into the regular comfort of the Fiat. My Fiat. The Ex-Mike Fiat. By the time I was seventeen and eligible to take my test the car was well and truly the property of Mr P Senior. Little P junior – embarrassed, disappointed and upset – was left to stew.

And stew I did. Instead of carrying out the plan I had hatched a year earlier (which involved taking my test as near to the stroke of midnight on my seventeenth birthday as test centre opening hours would allow), I acted as if learning to drive was the last thing on my mind. To prove that I was not hurt I

2

pushed all driving ambitions to the back of my mind. In fact, I made such a big deal of it not being a big deal that it wasn't until I was twenty-eight that I finally got round to learning how to drive.

But as well as being on foot for most of my late teens and twenties, I had also set up a few new rules about how I would go about things; I vowed that I wouldn't ever believe people when they made promises; I told myself to do whatever was necessary to avoid disappointment.

We've all had disappointments in life. Some of them have been the result of our own failings, while others have been caused by the let-downs of others. Whatever the story, coming face to face with the stark realisation that life isn't quite what we thought is common ground for us all.

Mary Magdalene knew about disappointment.

Then the disciples went back to their homes, but Mary stood outside the tomb crying. As she wept, she bent over to look into the tomb and saw two angels in white, seated where Jesus' body had been, one at the head and the other at the foot. They asked her, 'Woman, why are you crying?' 'They have taken my Lord away,' she said, 'and I don't know where they have put him.'

(John 20:10–13)

Mary was so upset, so gutted that all she could see was her own pain. 'They' had taken away *her* master. Perhaps there is even a note of self-pity creeping in there, but looking elsewhere in the Gospels it's clear that there is more to her than meets the eye. It is pretty much accepted that Mary Magdalene and Mary the sister of Martha were one and the same. In Luke 7:37 she is described as a 'woman who had lived a sinful life' – a polite way of calling her a prostitute or a woman who slept around. Jesus was probably the first man who had ever shown her true respect and dignity, who had loved her not for what he could get out of her, but simply to give to her. Jesus changed her life and gave her hope for the future. We see this in the retelling of her pouring the alabaster jar of expensive perfume all over Jesus' feet (John 12). She was so grateful to him that she would have given everything. I wonder if she ever thought that it was he who had already given everything for her.

Once Jesus had been crucified, everything changed for Mary. All her assumptions about life changed. She had spent most of her life as an outcast, confined to the fringes by polite society, but in Jesus she had found acceptance. Perhaps there had been a thought in the back of her mind that it may have been too good to be true, and with him now dead her worst fears had been realised. Kneeling before the empty tomb, peering in to see what had happened, Mary was too consumed by her own grief to notice that what she thought were guards were really angels. At this, she turned around and saw Jesus standing there, but she did not realise that it was Jesus.

'Woman,' he said, 'why are you crying? Who is it you are looking for?'

Thinking he was the gardener, she said, 'Sir, if you have carried him away, tell me where you have put him, and I will get him.'

(John 20:15)

Of course Jesus knew exactly who it was that she was looking for, but for Mary, the empty tomb represented a lifetime of hurt and disappointment; of let-downs, foul-ups and the fast-fading echoes of a promise that might have been but – so she thought – never was. So consumed was she with her own grief that she actually mistook Jesus – whose death acted as the trigger for her anguish – for the gardener. She wasn't having a very good day, yet all it took to turn it around was one word:

Jesus said to her, 'Mary.'

She turned towards him and cried out in Aramaic, 'Rabboni!' (which means Teacher).

Jesus said, 'Do not hold on to me, for I have not yet returned to the Father. Go instead to my brothers and tell them, "I am returning to my Father and your Father, to my God and your God." '

Mary Magdalene went to the disciples with the news: 'I have seen the Lord!' And she told them that he had said these things to her.

(John 20:17–18)

Many of us are kneeling in front of our own empty tombs; the pain of a divorce, a father who left us or a relationship that never worked out right. There may have been an accident or the pain may have been deliberate. It may have been a car that was never given or the realisation of wasted potential. We too can be so consumed with peering into these tombs of ours that we fail to recognise Jesus standing right by us. OK, so we may not actually be constantly hallucinating about gardeners, but you get my point, yes? It's all too easy to miss out on God when things are going wrong for us.

The answer? We need, like Mary, to hear him call our name. Then we need to embrace him, turning our focus from the tomb and placing it on him. Does that mean we should all be Black Belt Stiff Upper Lippers? No way – Jesus didn't take Mary from the cemetery right away, nor did he say, 'Cheer up, love.' No, there's a gap in the story that comes between Mary recognising Jesus and him saying, 'Let go, Mary.' Why let go? Because she was hugging him, right there and right then. He gave her permission to be genuine about her emotions with him, at the same time as presenting himself as the solution. That's what we need to be able to do too; to avoid the wallowing but not resist the welling-up. We need to be genuine, to allow the pain out, but also to look for the life on the other side of it all.

Of course all this can sound a little too easy, a little too trite and contrived – you know, just add water and all the pain will go away. Let's get it straight; that's not what this one's about. This book is about facing up to the real issues that present themselves to us as Christians and to those who aren't. We need to take a good long practical look at how Jesus – the risen saviour – can set us free from the disappointments, doubts, fears and brokenness of our lives.

> '**Out of our difficulties**
> **grow miracles.**'
> Jean de la Bruyère

2

Wasted Dreams
Joseph's Story

Over the years I have met a lot of Christians who have been characterised by one major trait: disappointment. I'm not talking about the wrong-sized socks at Christmas or a badly fitted filling, but real disappointment, the sort that stops you in your tracks, turning life a damp shade of grey. Why so? In almost all the situations that I'm thinking of, the disappointment is linked by a common theme: wasted dreams. To those of my friends who feel this way, nothing it seems is more draining of spiritual zeal than the failing of a dream.

But these people aren't alone, as I'm convinced that most of us go through at least one period where plans and aspirations appear to have come to nothing. We may have been fired up on inspired visions of tremendous works that we could do for the Lord, or perhaps we have been holding on to a promise that we believe came direct from God about how he would use us in the future. It may be that our plans were centred on having the ideal family unit – the cutely gap-toothed kids and the powerful estate on the driveway – or the ideal career combining money and power. This despair can affect us all, regardless of our beliefs. As the thinker Thoreau once said, most of us 'live lives of quiet desperation'.

But why do we go through these feelings? For many of us the reasons aren't so far beneath the surface as we might like to think. As time moves on and our bodies shuffle on from youth towards the inevitable, we are forced to replace the 'live forever' attitude of our younger days with a more measured 'pensions and central heating' orientated view of things. In short, we grow up, and that is the problem; for no one can dream dreams quite as magnificently as they did when they were a child.

Let's not limit ourselves to the middle-aged though. Just because they're called mid-life crises doesn't mean they come along only in the middle of our lives. I read a story about a public schoolboy who went missing from his room one day. His housemaster couldn't find him and, on questioning his friends, all he could find out was that the pupil had sold all his CDs just one week before. Eventually he came across a note. Fearing the worst, he read on. It went something like this:

> I've had enough. I can't take the pressure of knowing that my life is already mapped out in

front of me while I have no power to change it. Things are moving too fast and I have no time to think. I need time to think. I'll be back when I'm ready.

The boy – who had just completed his GCSEs the previous summer – had sold his music to buy a one-way ticket to Tobago. The note explained how he was going to fly out and meet up with a fisherman whom he had met while on holiday there a summer or two ago.

The reason why this story struck me as so interesting was because of the language of the note; feeling that time is running out, that life is all mapped out in front of you and that you are powerless to alter course is something that we associate far more often with middle-aged business people, weighed down by the burdens of finance and people. To hear them from a sixteen-year-old is – to say the least – unusual. But I know how he felt. The sensation of being trapped is never nice. Actually that's not entirely true; I once dreamt that I was trapped in a parallel universe where the currency was Sweet and Sour Pork and I was a millionaire. It wasn't so bad. What's so bad about feeling that you are trapped is when it comes double-packed with the belief that the future ahead of you is nothing like the future that you had previously been banking on. The schoolboy who did a bunk had probably spent years dreaming of freedom and good stuff. It's just a guess, but it's not hard to imagine how easy it would have been to get thrown off course by the thought of his future being made up of nothing more than years of never-ending pressures, whether study or work. Wasted dreams; there's nothing quite like them.

Thankfully the Bible has something to say about this. Actually that's a bit of an understatement, for through the story of Joseph we are given a close-up view of one of the most extreme cases of long-term disappointment that I can think of. Joseph not only had it tough; he also had been convinced that God had fantastic things in store for him. Watching the years trickle by from a prison cell in a foreign land, he could be forgiven for thinking that something had gone wrong somewhere. Joseph's story is a textbook example of how to endure the worst but still hang in there with God.

As the story opens we meet Joseph living in the town of Hebron with his eleven brothers and one sister.

> Joseph, a young man of seventeen, was tending the flocks with his brothers, the sons of Bilhah and the sons of Zilpah, his father's wives, and he brought their father a bad report about them. Now Israel loved Joseph more than any of his other sons, because he had been born to him in his old age; and he made a richly ornamented robe for him. When his brothers saw that their father loved him more than any of them, they hated him and could not speak a kind word to him.
>
> (Genesis 37:2–4)

And so we get the picture of the Golden Child syndrome. Joseph – favoured by his father Jacob (also called Israel) – obviously gets an easy time of it, staying at home with Dad while his brothers work hard with the flocks. Not only that but his dad (obviously with a good feel for what would and wouldn't work in late twentieth-century musicals) gives him an Amazing Technicoloured Dreamcoat, failing to do the same for the other eleven of his sons.

Understandably all this did very little to give the brothers a good opinion of Joseph, but if ever their affection for him was in question, it went right out of the window when they remembered how he had decided to give his dad 'a bad report about them', grassing them up for some offence or other.

However, these two offences were nothing compared with what came next. Joseph had a dream. Oh dear.

'Listen to this dream I had: We were binding sheaves of corn out in the field when suddenly my sheaf rose and stood upright, while your sheaves gathered around mine and bowed down to it.'

His brothers said to him, 'Do you intend to reign over us? Will you actually rule us?' And they hated him all the more because of his dream and what he had said.

Then he had another dream, and he told it to his brothers. 'Listen,' he said, 'I had another dream,

13

and this time the sun and moon and eleven stars were bowing down to me.'

When he told his father as well as his brothers, his father rebuked him and said, 'What is this dream you had? Will your mother and I and your brothers actually come and bow down to the ground before you?' His brothers were jealous of him, but his father kept the matter in mind.

(Genesis 37:6–11)

Joseph's arrogance and stupidity are plain to see, yet unfortunately the matter does not just end there. Up to this point in the Bible, it's clear to see that God had been in the habit of speaking to his people through various means about the future of the nation of Israel. He spoke to Abraham in a dream when he made his covenant with him and told him of the future of his new nation (Genesis 15:12–21), as well as to Jacob when he saw his ladder reaching to heaven (Genesis 28:10–15). So it makes sense that at this key point in Israel's formation (Jacob's twelve sons were the beginning of the twelve tribes of Israel) God would have a couple of things to say. Despite his monumental lack of tact and consideration for his brothers' feelings, Joseph was right; his dreams were from heaven. Eventually the contents of the dream were proved right, but not before Joseph's life seemed to take a massive detour.

As you probably know, things started to go wrong when Joseph was sent out by his father to find out how things were going with his brothers and their flocks. He travelled the thirty miles from Hebron to Shechem, only to discover that they had moved on a further twenty miles to the city of Dothan. Spotting him far off as he approached, his brothers plotted to kill him or at least arrange it so that he would be killed by a wild animal. Eventually Joseph ended up being sold as a slave to some travelling Midianite merchants on their way to Egypt.

Once in the foreign country – surrounded by unfamiliar people, language and customs – this good Jewish lad gets bought by Potiphar, a high-ranking official in Pharaoh's council. Due to some exceptionally good work on behalf of the young Israelite, Mr Potiphar takes a shine to Joseph and promotes him to the position of Chief Slave. Unfortunately he is not the only one who reckons that Joseph is worthy of attention, as Mrs Potiphar tries to seduce him. Deciding that a career as a gigolo was not quite what he had in mind, Joseph spurns Mrs P who convinces her husband that Joseph had tried to rape her. Soon Joseph is not only a slave in a foreign land, but an innocent prisoner too. Not quite the upright sheaf surrounded by bowing subjects.

In prison he meets a couple of Pharaoh's servants, the cupbearer and the baker. They tell him about a couple of dreams that they have had and Joseph asks God for the meaning. Delivering the interpretation that the baker will be executed and that the cupbearer will be released, he makes sure that the cupbearer agrees to remember Joseph once he's out and try his best to ensure his release.

On the third anniversary of his reign Pharaoh had a bit of a clear-out, hanging the baker and releasing the cupbearer, just as the dreams had been interpreted. 'The chief cupbearer, however, did not remember Joseph; he forgot him' (Genesis 40:23). Can you imagine Joseph's frustration and disappointment as he realised again that the interpretation of dreams that he thought were from God only ever seemed to lead him into trouble?

It takes a couple more years for the story to move on, when it's Pharaoh's turn to have a confusing dream. None of his sorcerers or magicians can work out the meaning behind the fat cows and the thin cows, but as the cupbearer remembers his old cell-mate, Joseph gets the call once again. Joseph could easily have given up at this point, saying that he didn't 'do dreams', that they just caused too much trouble. Instead he decides to ask God for the interpretation, which he duly receives and com-municates to a very grateful Pharaoh, who busts him out of jail and gives him the job of chancellor of the exchequer. Nice.

Of course Joseph's interpretation of the dream not only made sense at the time, it also outlined the precise way that things were going to happen; true to form there was a seven-year period of economic and agricultural boom which was followed by seven years of killer bust. The famine threatened the lives of Egypt's neighbours, but under the prudent eye of

Joseph, Pharaoh's stores had enough grain in them to ride it out.

So Israel's sons were among those who went to buy grain, for the famine was in the land of Canaan also. Now Joseph was the governor of the land, the one who sold grain to all its people. So when Joseph's brothers arrived, they bowed down to him with their faces to the ground. He played with his brothers for a while, who remained unaware of the true identity of the man they were dealing with.

Then Joseph could no longer control himself before all his attendants, and he cried out, 'Make everyone leave my presence!' So there was no-one with Joseph when he made himself known to his brothers. And he wept so loudly that the Egyptians heard him, and Pharaoh's household heard about it.

Joseph said to his brothers, 'I am Joseph! Is my father still living?' But his brothers were not able to answer him, because they were terrified at his presence.

Then Joseph said to his brothers, 'Come close to me.' When they had done so, he said, 'I am your brother Joseph, the one you sold into Egypt! And now, do not be distressed and do not be angry with yourselves for selling me here, because it was to save lives that God sent me ahead of you. For two years now there has been famine in the land, and for the next five years there will not be ploughing and reaping. But God sent me ahead of you to preserve for you a remnant on earth

and to save your lives by a great deliverance.'
(Genesis 45:1–7)

Joseph's story gets me for many reasons; I love the accuracy of his interpretations, the boldness with which he takes on the challenge of succeeding where Pharaoh's best had failed. But as well as those characteristics I love the fact that in many ways the story is so normal; he was stupid and arrogant when he was younger and then for years his life was not easy, the spiritual fireworks were not going off and Joseph looked every bit the failure. Yet he hung in there, and that gives me hope. Joseph didn't consider his life to be a waste simply because it hadn't progressed at the speed and in the order that he had hoped.

Too many of us get floored by the wasted years, months and even weeks – just one period of time where things don't seem to be heading in the right direction can be enough to send us back to apathetic mediocrity with our tail between our legs. Maybe it was a failed exam or a broken relationship, a change of family circumstance or a force way beyond your control. When things look as though they aren't going to work out quite the way we had thought, the temptation to give in can be great. It can be so much easier to write off an unfulfilled dream as a mistake or a waste than to risk the pain of patiently waiting for it to be fulfilled.

This wasn't on the menu for Joseph. He refused to get bitter, to consider all that had once sparked his hope to be false. He stuck with it and remained true to the dreams that God had given him. Instead of turning away from God he turned towards him, getting closer to him and depending on him. For proof of that just look at what the Scriptures have to say about the children born to Joseph while he was in Egypt:

> Joseph named his firstborn Manasseh and said, 'It is because God has made me forget all my trouble and all my father's household.' The second son he named Ephraim and said, 'It is because God has made me fruitful in the land of my suffering.'
>
> (Genesis 41:51–2)

Joseph faced questions and tests and so do we. It may not come down to being sold into slavery, but there will be plenty of chances for us to get the hump with God for not working things out to our precise specifications. Will we get bitter when this happens? Will we decide that God has got it wrong? Are we really that brave?

> 'For my thoughts are not your thoughts, neither are your ways my ways,' declares the Lord.
>
> (Isaiah 55:8)

Will we live a life in expectation of the fulfilment of God's promises? If so, I think it's a reasonably sound idea to get to grips with this verse from Isaiah – after all, God's ways can seem mighty strange at times. Funnily enough, though, they always seem to work out best.

It comes down to choice between our way and learning God's way. At the end of it all, faced with the sight of his brothers pleading with him for food, Joseph could easily have exacted a little sweet revenge for their treatment of him. It would have been so easy for him to have them taken away and 'dealt with'. But God had taught him a few lessons throughout his stay in the foreign land. He had taught Joseph about his sovereignty; reminding him that God was in charge. He dealt with Joseph's arrogance so that when his family finally did bow in front of him, Joseph didn't make a big deal of it. Joseph's first dream of sheaves bowing down before him finally came true over twenty-two years after he had it. Instead of sticking his tongue out he told them of God's plan, how he had been sent to serve them: 'God sent me ahead of you to preserve for you a remnant on earth and to save your lives by a great deliverance.'

Sometimes God delays fulfilling the dreams so that we might have enough time to learn valuable lessons. It may not just be arrogance that needs to get sorted within us; it may be that we need to recognise God's sovereignty over our own ability. Personally I had plenty of dreams that seemed to have got lost along the way. When I was fifteen I had sermons in me that I was convinced were going to spark huge revival worldwide. I would practise in front of the mirror, alternating between my light-hearted 'rolling in the aisles' delivery and my stern 'on your knees' calls to repentance. At times I was so convincing that I even went forward myself. Working as a second-rate accountant I wondered where it had all gone wrong. Each day I sat there, internally grieving the potential that I had been so convinced would one day be unleashed on a sinful world. I felt embarrassed and let down, worrying that all my zeal had gone to waste.

I had to wait. It was thirteen years before I got round to preaching, and in that time I figured out that there are two modes of waiting on offer. The first – and by far my favourite for most of my twenties – is waiting with your thumb in your mouth. 'Well God,' you say to yourself, 'I don't suppose you're ever going to use me.' The second – and what I found to be by far the most elusive – is to wait as Joseph did; expectantly. In the waiting he lived a faithful and obedient life, taking what opportunities he had to do God's will. Eventually this faithful young man got to see his early dreams fulfilled in ways that he could never have imagined before.

God doesn't want merely to use you for the sake of it – that's not why he gives us dreams and ambitions. God wants more than to just do stuff through you, he wants to do it *in* you. We have a saying in our church: we have to go deeper before we go further. The gap between getting the dreams and seeing them fulfilled is the time when it's up to us whether we go deeper with God. That way, when things are moving along nicely and he's taking us further along with him, fulfilling our dreams, we won't let him down.

'Faith is often strengthened right at the place of disappointment.'

Rodney McBride

'Your worst days are never so bad that you are beyond the reach of God's grace. And your best days are never so good that you are beyond the need of God's grace.'

Jerry Bridges

3

Wasted Potential
Samson's Story

While the thought of having to deal with a whole load of wasted dreams is not exactly a pleasant one, there is one thing that I find more tragic and disturbing: the worry that one day I may wake up believing that I have wasted my potential. I've seen it happen to some of my friends and my guess is that you will have seen the same; talented people, those with loads going for them who get tripped up by some kind of fatal flaw. Perhaps not quite as extreme as the story of ambitious Mr Macbeth, but these are people who somehow end up sacrificing their ability. Please don't get me wrong, I'm not condemning them or pointing the finger – there are plenty of things I do that get in the way of my relationship with God – I simply find it sad when our taste for the forbidden fruit gets in the way of the good things that God has in store. It might not be a fatal flaw that gets in our way though; sometimes the simple act of making wrong choices can alter our course, leading us towards disappointment instead of satisfaction. Whatever the reason, there's nothing quite as sad as the tombstone that reads 'He Had Potential'. Maybe I feel strongly about this because of all those 'Could Do Better' reports I got while at school, but I'm sure that God feels the same; urging us to put down the things that threaten to distract and destroy us.

Samson is a classic case of someone who was jampacked with potential, but who because of both character flaws and bad choices ended up far away from a glorious ending. His story starts in the Old Testament at a time when his people were in the middle of a long period of occupation by their enemies.

> Again the Israelites did evil in the eyes of the Lord, so the Lord delivered them into the hands of the Philistines for forty years.
>
> (Judges 13:1)

This whole thing of Israel's sin being followed by a period of occupation is part of a pattern that appears throughout the book of Judges. What happened was that the nation of Israel would sin and begin to worship idols, so God would place them under the control of one of their neighbours. These enemy nations would rule over them for some time until the Israelites repented of their sin and asked God to set them free. In stepped God, who would raise up a deliverer who would lead them out of slavery and back to freedom. Eventually however, the whole thing would happened again as they eventually wandered off and started worshipping their idols once more. This cycle is repeated throughout the book of Judges, and the story of Samson appears in the seventh and last of these cycles.

The opening verse mentions that the Israelites were 'delivered into the hands of the Philistines' – a particularly savage and warlike people with roots in Egypt.

A certain man of Zorah, named Manoah, from the clan of the Danites, had a wife who was sterile and remained childless. The angel of the Lord appeared to her and said, 'You are sterile and childless, but you are going to conceive and have a son. Now see to it that you drink no wine or other fermented drink and that you do not eat anything unclean, because you will conceive and give birth to a son. No razor may be used on his head, because the boy is to be a Nazirite, set apart to God from birth, and he will begin the deliverance of Israel from the hands of the Philistines.'

(Judges 13:2–5)

The deal with Nazirites was that they took a vow that they would separate themselves from much of the world in order to be of service to God. The word comes from the Hebrew verb *nazar*, which means 'to separate, to cut off'. It seems that God had a specific

27

task in mind too – and not a bad one at that – 'he will begin the deliverance of Israel from the hands of the Philistines.' Not bad for a foetus.

So we see that even from before his birth Samson had potential as well as some strict guidelines for him to follow. As a Nazirite he was forbidden to touch a dead body of any kind, drink alcohol or have any contact with grapes or to cut his hair. These rules helped to set him apart as well as to paint a powerful picture of our need for dependence on God. For example, that thing with the hair was actually quite radical; having long hair (and I mean really long – longer than the women of the day) in the Scriptures was a rather shameful thing for a man and was considered to be a sign of weakness. Nazirites openly displayed their weakness in this way, a clear statement that they were totally reliant on God for their strength. Unfortunately, Samson was just a little too good at showing his own weakness.

The early years were promising. We are told that 'he grew and the Lord blessed him, and the Spirit of the Lord began to stir him while he was in Mahaneh Dan, between Zorah and Eshtaol' (Judges 13:25). Having been born with a silver spoon in his mouth (the angel of the Lord bringing back the results of the pregnancy tests as well as outlining his CV), to have the Spirit of God brood over him must have made his parents believe that his place as firestarter to the delivery of Israel was in the bag.

Unfortunately things began to go wrong:

Samson went down to Timnah and saw there a young Philistine woman. When he returned, he said to his father and mother, 'I have seen a Philistine woman in Timnah; now get her for me as my wife.'

His father and mother replied, 'Isn't there an acceptable woman among your relatives or among all our people? Must you go to the uncircumcised Philistines to get a wife?'

But Samson said to his father, 'Get her for me. She's the right one for me.'

(Judges 14:1–3)

Timnah was a small town about four miles away from Samson's home in Zorah, and it is this first recording of a Samson away-day that gives us a clear picture of his weakness, particularly when it came to the *laydeees*.

The first thing to note is that Samson's decision to marry a Philistine woman was a big no-no. The fact that God would use this woman to bring down the Philistines does not condone the fact that Samson broke the rules. Instead it says far more about God's grace and ultimate sovereignty. Samson should have known better than to contravene God's explicit commandments that intermarriage between the Israelites and those from other nations was strictly off limits. The Old Testament explains that because of his love, God decreed that his people should marry within their own nationality. A member of an idolatrous people would pollute a good Israelite household, as well as being no fun for the 'foreigner'. It all feels a tad funny talking about 'racial purity' in this day and age (normally we leave that up to the bigoted fascists), but we need to take it in context; these were violent enemies and everything was at stake.

Samson, however, thought with his pants, stamping his feet and getting his own way when his parents questioned his decision. Living so close to Timnah and the territory of the Philistines is a useful picture of how Samson lived on the edge spiritually as well as physically. Instead of taking care he blustered his way through, putting self before God.

Before we judge him and put him on the scrapheap, it's vital to remind ourselves that God's ways are not our ways, and that he can still choose to use people despite their failings.

> Samson went down to Timnah together with his father and mother. As they approached the vineyards of Timnah, suddenly a young lion came roaring toward him. The Spirit of the Lord came upon him in power so that he tore the lion apart with his bare hands as he might have torn a young goat. But he told neither his father nor his mother what he had done.
>
> (Judges 14:5–6)

Just check out that power; ripping apart a lion as if it were a goat shows that Samson was seriously anointed.

Some time later, when he went back to marry her, he turned aside to look at the lion's carcass. In it was a swarm of bees and some honey, which he scooped out with his hands and ate as he went along. When he rejoined his parents, he gave them some, and they too ate it. But he did not tell them that he had taken the honey from the lion's carcass.

(Judges 14:8–9)

Oh dear. Not only did Samson make the mistake of touching a dead animal, he also was a bit sly in not telling his parents where the honey came from, so causing them to defile themselves by eating from an unclean animal. In fact, if you think about it, the whole thing's quite symbolic: he performed a spectacular act that gave glory to God, ripping apart flesh under the power of the Spirit. Later his fleshly appetites outweighed his spiritual resolve and he satisfied his hunger by munching on a parasite that had lived off the by-product of God's glory.

You have to question exactly what Samson was doing there in the first place. After all, his Nazirite vows forbade him touching not only wine, but grapes too. Pretty hard thing to avoid grapes in a vineyard. What's more, it's kind of strange that he would be poking around inside a lion's carcass anyway, especially when you add in the danger element of a swarm of bees being present. Altogether the picture pulls into focus and we conclude that Samson was wilfully and on many different counts trying to break God's laws. It wasn't as if he slipped up in a nanosecond; he broke through many barriers – the vineyard, the dead lion, the honey – in order to satisfy his appetite. Playing with fire, a life on the edge, call it what you will, Samson couldn't resist taking chances.

The risk-taking continues at his wedding. Samson provokes the Philistines by setting them a riddle, agreeing with them that – should they work it out within the seven days of the feast – he would give them 'thirty linen garments and thirty festal garments'. These were exceptionally expensive threads (a man might expect to own one in his entire lifetime) and Samson was setting himself up to give them each two. If they didn't get the solution then they were to give him two of the garments each, so there was a reasonable incentive for the Philistines to work it out and for Samson not to tell them. What was the riddle, you ask?

'Out of the eater, something to eat; out of the strong, something sweet.'

(Judges 14:14a)

Again he's walking a tightrope, referring to a secret miracle of God's, using it to line his own pocket.

For three days they could not give the answer.

On the fourth day, they said to Samson's wife, 'Coax your husband into explaining the riddle for us, or we will burn you and your father's household to death. Did you invite us here to rob us?'

Then Samson's wife threw herself on him, sobbing, 'You hate me! You don't really love me. You've given my people a riddle, but you haven't told me the answer.'

'I haven't even explained it to my father or mother,' he replied, 'so why should I explain it to you?'

She cried the whole seven days of the feast. So on the seventh day he finally told her, because she continued to press him. She in turn explained the riddle to her people.

(Judges 14:14b–17)

Once more we see Samson's inability to say no to the flesh. This time, however, instead of defiling his immediate family, he travels to Ashkelon (a coastal town thirty miles away) where he murders, loots and pillages until he has enough cash to pay back the now rather happy Philistines. It's a terrible story, made even more confusing by the fact that God appears to help him, as 'the Spirit of the Lord came mightily upon him' during the killing spree. With thirty men dead it's hard to see how God's hand could be on Samson's Great Escape, but I guess that's just the way things go; God sometimes does give us more than we deserve to help when we're up against a wall. One thing's for sure, I wouldn't like to expect God to do that sort of thing every time I messed up.

There followed a few more mess-ups, but eventually Samson ends up ruling the Israelites in peace for twenty years. That is until he makes a total hash of it all and takes a trip to Gaza, where he sleeps with a prostitute. Doh! What a chief. Twenty years of victory, twenty years of peace and he throws it all away for one night of sex. Remind you of anyone? In our own ways we all do it, I suppose; we all can taste the intimacy of a relationship with Jesus, all know that he really is all that we need to get by, but we chuck it away for a moment's gratification.

> The people of Gaza were told, 'Samson is here!' So they surrounded the place and lay in wait for him all night at the city gate. They made no move during the night, saying, 'At dawn we'll kill him.'
> (Judges 16:2)

Yet again the Lord is there for him, saving him miraculously by allowing him to escape through the Philistines at night and rip off the gates at the city wall, which he carries on his back the thirty-eight miles to Hebron. Then we read: 'Some time later, he fell in love with a woman in the Valley of Sorek whose name was Delilah' (Judges 16:4).

It's the same old pattern; he messes up, God helps him out. This time it's another pagan woman who catches his eye, Delilah (whose name in Hebrew means 'weak'). Not surprisingly considering the amount of grief that he has caused them over the years, the Philistines are quite keen on the idea of Samson being six foot under. The Philistine lords ask Delilah to find out the secret of his strength, offering to pay her 1,100 pieces of silver each should she comply, making the total purse 5,500 pieces of silver.

Of course Delilah cannot resist and sets about trying to discover the secret of his might. What follows is pure farce; immature Samson plays along with the gag by telling Delilah a lie about what makes him so powerful. Each time Delilah passes on the lie to the Philistines, who try out the theory on him at night. First they are told that if he is bound with fresh bowstrings he will be helpless. He isn't. Then they take his advice and try tying him up with new ropes, but these fail to hold him. Having been told that if seven locks of his hair were woven into a web he would be helpless, Delilah tries it but he wakes up, rips the loom right off the wall and walks out the door. Finally she tries a new tack:

'How can you say, "I love you," when you won't confide in me? This is the third time you have made a fool of me and haven't told me the secret of your great strength.'

(Judges 16:15)

He caves in, telling her:

'No razor has ever been used on my head . . . because I have been a Nazirite set apart to God since birth. If my head were shaved, my strength would leave me, and I would become as weak as any other man.'

(Judges 16:17)

35

Finally Samson has given up the last of his Nazirite vows. Succumbing to Delilah it doesn't take long for him to cave in and for the Philistines to capture him, gouge out his eyes, humiliate him and set him to work pushing a great millstone round and round (a task usually carried out by oxen).

Samson ends up in misery with his enemies laughing at both him and his God. I've known people who have ended up in almost similar situations, and in each situation, like Samson, it all starts with the little sins. Samson chose the wrong girl and had a sweet tooth, yet these were the seeds of his own destruction. Some of us have justified other things; a little greed, lust or selfishness can seem so trivial, so easy to forget about. Once they're done and we find that God still seems to be with us, that he still answers prayers and still seems to care about our lives, then the temptation can come to think that we have got away with it. And so we carry on, taking another bite at sin's apple, dulling our senses to the bitterness of its taste.

When Samson was finally caught by the Philistines and they gouged out his eyes, he lost not only his strength but his vision. We too can fall into that trap, as when our crimes catch us up we can lose that clarity which once made us so sure of where we were going.

While they were in high spirits, they shouted, 'Bring out Samson to entertain us.' So they called

Samson out of the prison, and he performed for them.

When they stood him among the pillars, Samson said to the servant who held his hand, 'Put me where I can feel the pillars that support the temple, so that I may lean against them.' Now the temple was crowded with men and women; all the rulers of the Philistines were there, and on the roof were about three thousand men and women watching Samson perform. Then Samson prayed to the Lord, 'O Sovereign Lord, remember me. O God, please strengthen me just once more, and let me with one blow get revenge on the Philistines for my two eyes.' Then Samson reached toward the two central pillars on which the temple stood. Bracing himself against them, his right hand on the one and his left hand on the other, Samson said, 'Let me die with the Philistines!' Then he pushed with all his might, and down came the temple on the rulers and all the people in it. Thus he killed many more when he died than while he lived.

(Judges 16:25–30)

For the first time in the whole of the record of Samson's life we read of him praying. Up until then he had been taking God's mercy for granted; there is no record of him spending time with the Lord, no record of him carrying out any of the spiritual disciplines. It was only at the eleventh hour, after he had repeatedly failed to do the right thing, that he finally wised up and cried out to God in his weakness. I think that last line is one of the saddest in the Old Testament; a mighty warrior with God on his side, his greatest battle was his last. In spiritual terms that means that in his death he did more good than he had managed to do in the whole of his life. What a life of wasted potential.

There are many of us who, on looking back over our Christian lives, will decide that the years are marked by wasted potential instead of well-used talents. Let's not do that, let's take every day and live it for Jesus, putting his agenda before our own, trying to go by his values instead of the world's. That's what living life to the max is all about, using your gifts and talents in the very best way. Let's not sit on them, longing to be a preacher when really our talents make us an administrator, or hoping for the break as a worship leader when really we're best at caring for people and giving them time and love. As well as making sure we're making the right choices, we need to get down on our knees before God, making sure we're in the right place, that instead of sin we're marked by holiness.

As Oscar Schindler weeps at the end of *Schindler's List*, mourning all the things he could have done to save even more people, I always fell like shouting, 'but you have done so much'. One of my biggest fears is that I'll end up weeping for the things I never did and that there won't be anything to show for my life. I don't want that, I want to live the life God's given me to the full. I want to enjoy every last drop of life that's in my body, and that means staying close to him, following him, learning to adore him more. Wasted potential may be a terrible thing, but it's not the only thing on the menu; there's plenty more to choose from.

'The ultimate measure of a man is not where he stands in moments of comfort and convenience, but where he stands at times of challenge and controversy.'

Martin Luther King Jr

4

When Bad Things Happen to Good People

Job's Story

I suppose my only real claim to fame is that my brother once sold Lady Diana a pair of tights. (OK, so it might not be much, but it's all I've got.) It happened when both of us little Pilavachi boys worked at Harvey Nichols (pronounced *Harvey Nicks, Darling*) in Knightsbridge; Peter downstairs on Tights For Royalty and me upstairs in the slightly less glamorous Accounts department. For seven years I pushed paper and worked hard towards my eventual accreditation as World's Worst Accountant. Quite an achievement, I think you'll agree, and I'm glad to say in all humility that I fully deserved it.

When I started the job I was introduced to the rest of the department personnel, and quickly worked out the particular dynamics of the office. I say quickly, as working out the personality types on offer in a room full of accountants is not exactly the hardest job in the world. One person that did get my attention though, was Pat. She was the nicest person in the office, and it was clear that everybody else agreed. Not only was she kind, generous and caring, but she always seemed to have a smile on her face and was ready to chat and be interested in whatever anyone told her. Pat was one of those gold-dust characters who enhance the life of a place simply by their presence.

But there was a history that lay behind Pat which was at odds with the smile. I knew, mainly because people avoided talking about it, that she had been through some difficult times in her past. One day my colleagues told me. A few years previously Pat had been diagnosed as having cancer of the lymph gland, and many thought she was going to die. Against the odds she had managed to pull through, although as a result she was left unable to have children. They told me about her husband, Jan – a first generation Hungarian who worked hard in a factory. They were very much in love and, because of the cancer, they knew that all they had in the world was each other. My colleagues told me how traumatic her encounter with cancer had been, but that it was in remission and for the previous few years she and Jan had been rebuilding their lives together.

One day she didn't look so well. The days turned into weeks and the weeks into months, and Pat continued to deteriorate. After one of her regular check-ups she found out that the cancer was back. They tried the same treatment as before, but slowly she seemed to get worse. Eventually she stopped coming to work and the next time that I saw her was when we visited her in hospital. What I saw shocked me; she was in a terrible state, and both she and Jan knew it. They both cried and I couldn't handle it. I didn't visit again. One month later she died. She loved and wanted children, but she left none behind. Jan was left alone in a foreign country. We all asked, 'Why her?' Of all of us in the department Pat was the last person to deserve so early and tragic a death.

The biggest question that we can ask God is: 'Why?' Eventually most of us take our turn to do so, as throughout life we all encounter trauma and tragedy. It is then we find out that somehow the answers that seem so valid when things are going well appear appropriate and unsatisfactory. The truth was that for us, there was no answer to the question, 'Why Pat?' As a Christian that confusion took on a different twist for me from that of many of my colleagues, and it stayed with me for years to come.

I'm reminded of Pat whenever I hear about the casualties of earthquakes or other 'natural' disasters. When harmless civilians are killed, the weak are exploited or lives are claimed by epidemics, when I'm reminded of how it seems that it is always the innocent that suffer the most, I cannot help but ask, 'Why?'

There have been a few people throughout the ages who have resisted this urge to question the Almighty.

Considering it blasphemy or a lack of respect, they have tried to gloss over the issue of suffering by encouraging people to concentrate on the good rather than the bad. While I'm all in favour of a bit of positive thinking, I cannot help but think that this attitude does more harm than good. I believe that we all need to search for answers, in much the same way that I believe we need to grieve at the loss of a loved one. Treating funerals as celebrations of the life passed away can deny our need to mourn and say goodbye. Yes, the person may have gone to a better place, but ours is a sadder place for their passing. It's the same with suffering; yes, God is in charge, he does see the bigger picture, but we do people a disservice when we tell them that asking about suffering is a no-go area.

As Christians we believe that God is all-powerful, as well as being all-good. Take that line of reason and it's not long before you find yourself being asked, 'Well, if God is all-powerful he should be *able* to stop suffering. If he is all-good, he should *want* to stop suffering.' The logical conclusion would be, 'In that case, which one isn't he: all-powerful or all-good?'

When I was at school I had trouble with maths. It made little sense and try as I might, I just couldn't seem to get my head around it. Worse of all, though, was algebra. All that stuff about $x+y=2(y-z)$ had me scratching my head till the page disappeared under a flurry of dry scalp. That kind of mental block is familiar to many of us out of the classroom too, especially when it comes to the million-dollar question: why do bad things happen to good people?

Actually, it's not only good people that bad things happen to, and I feel that now is the time to tell you about Louis and Albert. Some time ago I decided that I needed a pet. I gathered my friends about me and held lengthy discussions about precisely what type of animal would be suitable for a disorganised, travelling young man such as myself. A dog was too much commitment and the fact that my flat is on the third floor ruled out a cat. I've killed more fish by overfeeding than I think is healthy and I don't like hamsters as they give me the creeps. Then I met Louis and Albert. Actually, I first met Sergeant Jenkins, a beautiful macaw parrot, but it all seemed a bit much so the pet shop owner took me to the budgie section where Louis and Albert introduced themselves. I was sold, and so were they, and the three of us returned home to start our new life together.

I fed them every day, talked with them constantly and would even phone up and talk to them over the answerphone while I was away just so that they didn't get too lonely without me. It was a wonderful time for all of us.

One day I returned home to find Louis lying belly-up on the floor of the cage. Wondering whether he was merely sleeping I tried to wake him, but it soon became clear that this was one nap that he would not be waking up from. He was dead, kaput, an ex-budgie – and I was distraught. The funeral was brief but heartfelt, and Albert and I tried our best to piece things together as a twosome. To be honest, he was a real rock at the time, and I suspect the strain of having to be strong for me was a deciding factor in his own death, barely a week later. Again I found him belly-up on the floor of the cage, and this time I knew that this signalled the end of Albert's brief time on this earth. What had they done to deserve it?

There's a book of the Bible that is written to answer that very question (although not specifically about budgies). Like my algebra problems, however, the answer at the end of it is very different from the one that we may have anticipated at the beginning.

Job (along with Psalms, Proverbs, the Song of Songs and Ecclesiastes) is part of the poetry section of the Bible. That means it was written with a purpose but also with a little creative imagination. Some people don't believe that there ever really was a person named Job – or at least if there was, that his story didn't follow quite the same script as we see in the Bible – but whether it is true or metaphorical, I am convinced that God inspired the writing of Job in order to speak to us about this whole question of suffering.

In Job we come face to face with someone whose suffering was grotesque. It was even worse than the suffering endured by my friend Pat, and at times it all can seem too much. We pick it up at the beginning:

In the land of Uz there lived a man whose name was Job. This man was blameless and upright; he feared God and shunned evil. He had seven sons and three daughters, and he owned seven thousand sheep, three thousand camels, five hundred yoke of oxen and five hundred donkeys, and had a large number of servants. He was the greatest man among all the people of the East.

(Job 1:1–3)

What a beginning; Job had it all. Not only was he wealthy financially, but he had a thriving family and a spot-on relationship with God. David Beckham, after having won the treble in 1999 with Manchester United as well as becoming a father for the first time, said, 'Life doesn't get better than this; I've got everything I want and I couldn't ask for more.' He could have nicked the line from Job, for the Old Testament figure was pretty much about as happy as it was possible to get.

Job was such a top fella in the eyes of the Lord that whenever his sons had a party, Job would make an offering to his God just in case his kids had sinned and cursed God in their hearts. Talk about holy; the guy was even atoning for sins that hadn't happened.

After the scene has been set things turn a little bizarre:

'One day the angels came to present themselves before the Lord, and Satan also came with them. The Lord said to Satan, "Where have you come from?"'

(Job 1:6–7a)

Excuse me! What the heck is all that about? I mean, Satan wandering around heaven, bold as brass, chatting with God. It's just plain weird.

> Satan answered the Lord, 'From roaming through the earth and going to and fro in it.'
> Then the Lord said to Satan, 'Have you considered my servant Job? There is no-one on earth like him; he is blameless and upright, a man who fears God and shuns evil.'
>
> (Job 1:7b–8)

The picture we get of this cosy little scene is God bragging to Satan about how much of a good old boy Mr Job is. 'See my boy Job?' you could translate it, 'Well, he's rock 'ard.'

> 'Does Job fear God for nothing?' Satan replied. 'Have you not put a hedge around him and his household and everything he has? You have blessed the work of his hands, so that his flocks and herds are spread throughout the land. But stretch out your hand and strike everything he has, and he will surely curse you to your face.'
>
> (Job 1:9–11)

According to Satan, Job's only as 'upright and blameless' as he is because God has been on his side. He is accusing God of having a follower who is only loyal as long as the sun is shining and the blessings are flowing. And as you can imagine, this kind of fighting talk cannot go ignored and God agrees to the challenge with the strict proviso that while he can do whatever he wants to his wealth, Satan cannot lay a finger on Job.

> One day when Job's sons and daughters were feasting and drinking wine at the oldest brother's house, a messenger came to Job and said, 'The oxen were ploughing and the donkeys were grazing nearby, and the Sabeans attacked and carried them off. They put the servants to the sword, and I am the only one who has escaped to tell you!'
>
> (Job 1:13–15)

Ouch!

> While he was still speaking, another messenger came and said, 'The fire of God fell from the sky and burned up the sheep and the servants, and I am the only one who has escaped to tell you!'
>
> (Job 1:16)

That hurts.

> While he was still speaking, another messenger came and said, 'The Chaldeans formed three raiding parties and swept down on your camels and carried them off. They put the servants to the sword, and I am the only one who has escaped to tell you!'
>
> (Job 1:17)

Again, not exactly 'good news'.

> While he was still speaking, yet another messenger
> came and said, 'Your sons and daughters were
> feasting and drinking wine at the oldest brother's
> house, when suddenly a mighty wind swept in from
> the desert and struck the four corners of the house.
> It collapsed on them and they are dead, and I am
> the only one who has escaped to tell you!'
>
> (Job 1:18–19)

Oh dear.

All it took was a few moments and Job's wonderful
life was wiped off the board. Not only his wealth,
but his family too – that's a pretty hard blow to
recover from. I know how I'd react, and I'm sorry to
say that it would be nothing like Job's response:

> At this, Job got up and tore his robe and shaved
> his head. Then he fell to the ground in worship
> and said: 'Naked I came from my mother's womb,
> and naked I will depart. The Lord gave and the
> Lord has taken away; may the name of the Lord
> be praised.' In all this, Job did not sin by charging
> God with wrongdoing.
>
> (Job 1:20–2)

That is incredible. To be able to see the Lord so
clearly through tragedy, to have such maturity in the
midst of so great a tragedy is something I can only
dream of achieving. But that's not the end of it, as

once again we see Satan taking a stroll around heaven. Bumping into God a bit of the old familiar chat starts up as God teases him for not being able to throw his protégé off balance. 'Ah,' says Satan, 'that's because you wouldn't let me trouble him physically. Now if Job got sick, then he'd turn his back on his God.'

> The Lord said to Satan, 'Very well, then, he is in your hands; but you must spare his life.'
> So Satan went out from the presence of the Lord and afflicted Job with painful sores from the soles of his feet to the top of his head. Then Job took a piece of broken pottery and scraped himself with it as he sat among the ashes.
>
> (Job 2:6–8)

What a horrific picture; the most upright and blameless man in the whole of Egypt and he's cutting himself with broken pottery to get relief from the sores that cover his body. His wife – probably like most of us – questions his sanity: 'His wife said to him, "Are you still holding on to your integrity? Curse God and die!" ' (Job 2:9). But for the second time he hits back with a home-run of spiritual maturity: 'He replied, "You are talking like a foolish woman. Shall we accept good from God, and not trouble?" In all this, Job did not sin in what he said' (Job 2:10).

I'm not sure how things work for you, but I feel reasonably confident that my faith in God can stand up to certain testing – bereavement, stress and worry – but as soon as my health goes, I'm in trouble. It can be as insignificant as a mild headache, but it can be enough to have me growling, spitting and generally getting ready to renounce my faith. A cold is not something to be kept to myself, instead I make a point of telling as many people as possible how cursed I am and try to bleed people of every last drop of sympathy they have going. In short, I am a nightmare, and compared to what Job went through, I am a worm. No matter what the devil threw at him, Job remained faithful to God and refused to throw in the towel on a relationship that was beginning to show him the extremes of human experience.

Any similarity between me and Job is limited to the fact that we both had visitors. While mine generally don't stick around for long, Job's three bearers of grapes and advice spent a considerable amount of time at his bedside.

> When they saw him from a distance, they could hardly recognise him; they began to weep aloud, and they tore their robes and sprinkled dust on their heads. Then they sat on the ground with him for seven days and seven nights. No-one said a word to him, because they saw how great his suffering was.
>
> (Job 2:12–13)

Yes, you guessed it; they were just the sort of visitors you don't need when you're ill. For the next thirty-six chapters the three visitors discussed with the patient every aspect of his affliction, trying wherever possible to be helpful. They weren't. As Job bemoans his very existence, Eliphaz the Temanite, Bildad the Shuhite and Zophar the Naamathite try their best to offer explanations for his predicament. They suggest that his suffering is a result of sin, but they are wrong. Suffering does not always indicate wrongdoing; if only it did we wouldn't even be bothering with a chapter like this.

So while the three chaps are busy trying to persuade Job to confess to a crime that he didn't commit, you could be forgiven for wondering what God was up to. In truth God is silent for the vast majority of the book, allowing the visitors to fill it with a whole load of misinformed nonsense. Finally, God speaks in Job 38: 'Then the Lord answered Job out of the storm. He said: "Who is this that darkens my counsel with words without knowledge? Brace yourself like a man; I will question you, and you shall answer me"' (Job 38:1–3).

It's as if the Lord suddenly brings the place down. 'Who are you to question me?' he asks. It's his job to do the asking, not that of foolish men. God didn't come to give Job answers, but to ask things of him … 'Where were you when I laid the earth's foundation? Tell me, if you understand. Who marked off its dimensions? Surely you know!' (Job 38:4–5).

The hint of sarcasm helps to show us just how ridiculous it is for Job and friends to be questioning their Maker. God reinforces the point: 'Will the one who contends with the Almighty correct him? Let him who accuses God answer him!' (Job 40:2).

Finally Job realises his place: 'I am unworthy – how can I reply to you? I put my hand over my mouth. I spoke once, but I have no answer – twice, but I will say no more' (Job 40:4–5).

God replies with his second questioning of his servant: 'Would you discredit my justice? Would you condemn me to justify yourself?' (Job 40:8).

Do you see what God has done? In asking Job where he was when the earth was being made he is accusing him of discrediting the Lord's power. In asking him whether he would 'discredit his justice', he is accusing Job of not believing in his goodness. Ring any bells? The twin doubts of, 'Is God really powerful enough to help?' and 'Is he really good enough to care?' are heard not only today, but they have been around since the earliest days of humanity.

This part of the story gives us an interesting insight into God's response to these two doubts about his nature. It's clear that in this case God sees them as a little more than just questions – please be clear that the Bible isn't suggesting that asking questions of God is wrong – and that they have become more like condemnation. As God said, was Job trying to condemn him to justify his own self? We can be guilty of exactly this same attitude; we write God off as being too low on power or love to make a difference, and we use the argument to justify all manner of bad deeds. Take wars for example; we allow them to carry on, pulling the trigger ourselves as a nation or people group, and then ask God why he doesn't intervene. Sometimes the buck really does stop with us, and it doesn't take a genius to work out that most suffering on this earth can be traced back to the human race.

Finally Job responds:

> I know that you can do all things; no plan of yours can be thwarted. You asked, 'Who is this that obscures my counsel without knowledge?' Surely I spoke of things I did not understand, things too wonderful for me to know. You said, 'Listen now, and I will speak; I will question you, and you shall answer me.' My ears had heard of you but now my eyes have seen you.
>
> (Job 42:2–5)

This incredible ending leads us right back to the answer to the question 'Why?' Job at last realises that there is a bigger picture, one that he can neither fully see nor fully comprehend. Too many of us in our enlightened, scientific post-modern age treat God like we would any other lab experiment. We want to shove him under a microscope, prod him, dissect him and pull him apart for explanations. 'Is he worth following?' we ask ourselves. 'Only if he comes up to our high standards and expectations', comes our self-inflated reply. Actually there is a mystery that surrounds suffering, and many of the answers we won't even understand. But more important than our question of 'Why' is God's question to us: 'Will you hang in there, even though you don't understand?'

Job finally sussed that one out. He knew that we are not capable of understanding fully the reasons behind suffering and, after all, if God really is God, shouldn't there be a few things up his sleeve that we cannot quite grasp? Will we choose to turn away, angered by the affront to our own ego that God should inflict such pain on us, or will we press on with him? We weren't there when he created the world, and we certainly don't have knowledge on all the mysteries surrounding him, but thankfully it's not about knowledge; it's about trust. The only answer that works for me when things are going badly are Job's words: 'My ears had heard of you but now my eyes have seen you' (Job 42:5).

When I think of Pat I still don't have an answer to the 'Why?' question. This side of heaven I'm sure I will always be perplexed about the reasons why she died. But in the meantime, I do have an answer, one that keeps me in the best place for me; the answer is God. My ears had heard of him, but it wasn't until I saw suffering that my eyes saw him too. Pat's death showed me more of God; his suffering, his determination and, yes, his love and his power.

It is important to remember that while we're trying to take responsibility for our own part in suffering, we must not fall into the trap of thinking that God stands apart from it, aloof and uncaring. This is what I mean about seeing God in Pat's suffering; you see, Jesus suffered on the cross. He went through agony, through hell itself, and there is no pain that he has not felt. God is not oblivious to our pain, he sent his Son to share ours with us. But why, you may ask, if that is so, doesn't God simply take our suffering away? Wouldn't it be better all round if he did?

The story of Job contains our answer; do we wait until we understand the mystery before we bow the knee, or do we choose to be satisfied with God in the present? God makes clear which line of action he endorses.

Of course, there's one problem with Job's story; real or not, he was just a guy who got caught up in some wider and slightly bizarre goings-on. There happens to be another character in the Old Testament who was a prophet and who was actively trying to do God's will. In allowing Jeremiah to suffer, God ran the risk of sabotaging his own plans, yet again we get involved with a story where suffering was no stranger to one of God's people.

Jeremiah was called to be a prophet when he was just a child, and grew up in one of the most difficult times of Judah's history. His career spanned four decades and he prophesied over the last five of Judah's kings. The prophecies kicked off just before the people were about to be exiled from their country after a period of intense sin. Unfortunately they chose to ignore Jeremiah's words and their immediate fate was sealed.

Yet Jeremiah remained faithful to his God. Not that that was easy, you understand, as throughout his life Jeremiah went through some serious suffering: the first two kings who he prophesied over and liked were exiled and put to death (Jeremiah 22:10; 22:15). He was persecuted (15:15–19), plotted against (11:18–23), imprisoned (20:2), slandered (26:11), imprisoned again (37:14–15) and, most humiliating of all, was thrown down a cistern (38:4–6). He ended up in a terrible state as the events took their toll on him both emotionally and physically. They called him the 'weeping prophet' and the other book he wrote was called the Lamentations of Jeremiah. In Jeremiah 8:18 he despairs of comfort and in Jeremiah 13:17 he wants to break into tears for Judah. Jeremiah 9:2 sees him wanting to abandon Judah to her fate, and by Jeremiah 15:10 he wishes he had never been born. God comes in for a bit of stick as Jeremiah accuses him of wronging him (20:7) as do other people when he wants to get even with his 'tormentors' (18:19–23). Not only does he have to contend with this level of suffering, but he also has to deal with the anger and frustration welling up within. Yet he hung in there with God. Jeremiah poured out his heart and his pain before God, which is precisely what kept him going.

He may have been slightly short on answers, but Jeremiah the broken man carried on doing God's will because he never allowed his pain to get in the way of his relationship with his Lord and Saviour. Sadly, I've met Christians who haven't done the same; their pain has got in the way and instead of feeding off God, they have followed a path that has taken them further from him, the only true source of comfort for all of us.

What are we feeding off? There really only is a choice of two; either we feed off our problems or we turn to God. Choosing to focus purely on our pain and resentment will only ever lead to bitterness. Choosing to turn to God does not mean ignoring the pain, but it does mean putting him before it. As Job and Jeremiah discovered, our God is bigger than our suffering. Following God does not mean a free pass around suffering, it's actually far more likely to lead us towards it. For God, you see, is mysterious. But he is good, and he is powerful. It all comes down to where you draw the line; is there a heaven and eternal life? If this earth is all we believe that we've got, then of course suffering can seem like such a waste. If there is a God-given life after death, the suffering we encounter here on earth gets put in a distinctly different perspective. Where's your line in the sand?

'When the storms of life strike, it's what happens in you that determines what happens to you.'

Jerry Saville

'Trials are medicines which our gracious and wise Physician prescribes because we need them; and he proportions the frequency and weight of them to what the case requires. Let us trust his skills and thank him for his prescription.'

Sir Isaac Newton

5

When We Mess Up
David's Story

Over the years, I'm sure I've noticed a change in what newspapers choose to cover. Every time I turn a page now it seems as though I'm confronted by another revelation about the slip-ups and let-downs of some high-profile personality. From politicians to clergy, media stars to family doctors, it looks like there's an army of skeletons waiting to fight their way out of the closet and onto the front page. Not so when I was young; all I ever seemed to notice were pictures of Olivia Newton-John.

Even as I'm writing this the papers are full of stories about libel trials and the fall from grace of one of politics' more flamboyant stars. It was all this kind of sleaze that helped bring down the Tory government in the 1997 election, and much the same kind of muck that ruined the careers of numerous American TV evangelists and dodgy politicians.

People ask whether this will ever end, whether truth and honesty will ever be the norm again.

I'm afraid I've got news for those people yearning for the glory days of the distant past; it's always been this way. People have always sinned, slipped up and made an almighty hash of this thing called life. Want proof? Just look at the Bible.

Before we do though, let's get a few things straight. People say that there are three categories into which our common failings fall. First is money; the desire to acquire. When things are put above people in terms of importance, this can have serious side effects for those we have trampled on to get to our treasure. Second is sex; the appetites of the flesh. History has been littered with the exploits of Valentinos who have stopped at nothing to satisfy their selfish urges. Finally there's power; the desire to dominate. Whether it's in a relationship or over a whole population, the lust that some have for power has been the driving force behind oppression the world over. But let's not get too smug; if we're honest, we're all capable of falling. If we're really honest, we've all slipped up already. Is there a way back from these mistakes? How can we avoid them in the first place?

If there's one character in the Bible who understood the twin tastes of success and failure, it's David: from humble shepherd boy then anointed to be king of Israel, back to humble shepherd boy and then to slayer of Goliath and saviour of the nation. Then there's all that stuff when he's on the run from Saul, the wars and the torment. Finally we catch up with him in middle age, nicely settled as king over the nation he has defended for so long.

> In the spring, at the time when kings go off to war, David sent Joab out with the king's men and the whole Israelite army. They destroyed the Ammonites and besieged Rabbah. But David remained in Jerusalem.
>
> (2 Samuel 11:1)

And this is where it all goes wrong. David's mistake is clear to see. Instead of going off to fight as was the custom, David decides to take it easy and sit this particular battle out at home. He stopped doing what he was supposed to be doing as a king and left himself wide open to attack.

I remember the leader of the Vineyard church, John Wimber, once said that he didn't have time to sin as he was too busy serving the Lord. Hearing that sort of thing is enough to cause me to have a seizure. Does this mean we're all supposed to fill every spare moment of the day with 'Christian' work, look knackered and have no social lives? Having thought about it, I feel better. I don't think that's quite what he was getting at, but I do believe he had hit on a truth; you see, the more time I have doing absolutely nothing, the more I seem to sin. Once I forget about what I'm supposed to be doing (keeping my mind focused on Jesus), it's easy to get down to all that other stuff. Obviously we all need rest, relaxation and plenty of time to enjoy ourselves – without those good things we miss out on much that God has given us – but if, like David, we forget about what we've been called to do, things could easily turn sour.

> One evening David got up from his bed and walked around on the roof of the palace.
>
> (2 Samuel 11:2a)

So we see David taking it easy, having a quick snooze before dinner perhaps. There he is, just mooching around the place trying to soak up the time.

> From the roof he saw a woman bathing. The woman was very beautiful, and David sent someone to find out about her.
>
> (2 Samuel 11:2b–3a)

A mere coincidence that he should see a woman bathing? Rubbish! He was in a prime position for perving and he knew exactly what he wanted to get in his sights. He was gagging for it and what's more, he obviously didn't just turn away after his first glance, he made sure he had a good look at her. Then he took it further, sending someone to find out about her.

> The man said, 'Isn't this Bathsheba, the daughter of Eliam and the wife of Uriah the Hittite?' Then David sent messengers to get her.
>
> (2 Samuel 11:3b–4a)

Even when he found out that she was married – and to one of his soldiers – he still pursued his urges and had her delivered to his room where he slept with her.

> Then she went back home. The woman conceived and sent word to David, saying, 'I am pregnant.'
> (2 Samuel 11:4b–5)

Not good, huh? David had landed himself in it big time, and was surely about to run the risk of facing a serious drop in his approval rating. But it gets worse. Instead of owning up, confessing and opting for a clean start, David wades even further out into the sewage of his own mistakes. He abused the power of his kingship, called Uriah to come and see him and eventually sent him out to the front line, having given the order to all the other troops to withdraw. Stranded, Uriah was defenceless and was killed in battle. In order to make space for his sin, David compounded his adultery with murder, ending up a wretched and miserable man.

Yet God had mercy on him. He sent David a prophet by the name of Nathan, who told him this story.

> There were two men in a certain town, one rich and the other poor. The rich man had a very large number of sheep and cattle, but the poor man had nothing except one little ewe lamb that he had bought. He raised it, and it grew up with him and

his children. It shared his food, drank from his cup and even slept in his arms. It was like a daughter to him.

Now a traveller came to the rich man, but the rich man refrained from taking one of his own sheep or cattle to prepare a meal for the traveller who had come to him. Instead, he took the ewe lamb that belonged to the poor man and prepared it for the one who had come to him.

(2 Samuel 12:1b–4)

David was furious. Any man who would do such a thing should be punished by death. He must have been a bit sleepy as he didn't quite get the point of the story. Thankfully Nathan spelled it out for him:

You are the man! This is what the Lord, the God of Israel, says: 'I anointed you king over Israel, and I delivered you from the hand of Saul. I gave your master's house to you, and your master's wives into your arms. I gave you the house of Israel and Judah. And if all this had been too little, I would have given you even more. Why did you despise the word of the Lord by doing what is evil in his eyes? You struck down Uriah the Hittite with the sword and took his wife to be your own. You killed him with the sword of the Ammonites. Now, therefore, the sword will never depart from your house, because you despised me and took the wife of Uriah the Hittite to be your own.'

(2 Samuel 12:7–10)

What an amazing passage. That line about how much God had given him and how he would have given him even more does me in. They are the words of a father to a son, tender, generous and kind. Yet David took something that wasn't his; the world was not enough.

This is a familiar scenario for many of us. We too can seem to have it all – the giftings, the friendships, the opportunities to be satisfied and fulfilled – yet we can't keep our fingers away from the things that do not belong to us. Somehow things are never enough and we are left wanting whatever we think shines brighter than the treasure in our own possession. We can be like magpies, just in the same way that David was. Something catches our attention and that's the end of the story: we simply have to have it. The 'it' in question can be anything at all, from material possessions to satisfaction to influence, the three sides of the money–sex–power triangle.

When he was the richest man in the world, John Paul Getty was asked how much money he needed to be happy. 'Just a little bit more,' he replied. It's true, we cannot resist the urge within us to chase after the things that do not belong to us.

When David was told by Nathan that God knew about his sin, he repented. It wasn't just a quick 'Sorry, God' either, but one of the most heartfelt pleas in the Bible. What caused this change of heart? It could only have been one thing: the word of God. It wasn't down to clever arguments or a cunning trap to bring David back to his knees before his Creator, but the perspective of divine truth. For me too, I know that when I come into contact with God's word – whether through the Bible or a prophecy – it can often cause the most radical turn around in my life. Knowing that God knows about us, that he cares and wants to guide us is reason enough to follow his lead.

We need to keep listening out for God's voice. If we're not there's a real danger that we, like David, will become blind to the sins and potential pitfalls that lie in our path. I'm sure that's what happened, that David rationalised his fall bit by bit without ever really seeing the whole picture. After all, he had probably been going off to war every spring for years and felt like he deserved a rest. Perhaps we might feel similarly if we'd been reading our Bibles and praying every day for months. Maybe a big chunk of regular attendance at church might be traded for 'Well, I'll just take a few weeks off'. It might be that we've been doing well with giving money to the poor – 'Just a little bit spent on myself instead won't hurt.' At the beginning none of these seem like a big deal; of course it was OK for David to take it easy at home one season, of course God isn't going to burn you up for missing a few days' quiet times or church visits. And after all, you did work hard for that cash. Of course none of these are so wrong but, like David, the stopping of doing good things can so easily become the starting point for doing bad things.

While one thing was leading to another, David was busy making excuses every step of the way. Standing on the roof checking out a fine-looking lady, well, why couldn't he find out her name? After all, he was the king. So what if she's Uriah's wife? A little fun won't hurt. Once Bathsheba is pregnant David even manages to excuse murder in an attempt to cover his back. Little lies can lead to bigger lies, and without something stopping them, their momentum can increase at an alarming rate.

We know that God forgave David, but it is also clear that he had to live with the consequences of his actions for the rest of his life. The son born to Bathsheba was ill and David pleaded with God for his child's life, yet the boy died. David was forced to live with this grief from that point on, much in the same way that there are consequences to be paid whenever we mess up too. It's not all gloom though, for when David turned and said sorry to God, the Almighty had mercy on him, not only forgiving him but restoring his relationship with him.

We Christians can get very confused, particularly when it comes down to this whole issue of sin and consequences. Because we know that Jesus died to pay for our sins, we assume that somehow wiping out the consequences of our actions gets thrown in with the bargain. Unfortunately this wasn't the case for David and it certainly isn't the case for us. The scars may stay with us, but like David we won't be kept at arm's length by a cold and uncompassionate God. Look back at Psalm 51:1–3:

Have mercy on me, O God, according to your unfailing love; according to your great compassion blot out my transgressions. Wash away all my iniquity and cleanse me from my sin. For I know my transgressions, and my sin is always before me.

David knows the truth about his deeds – that his sin has placed a barrier between him and God. Only his Creator has the power to tear it down and the mercy to welcome David back into his presence. He's right, too, about his sins being always before him, about it always being around to remind him. He was surrounded by the litter of his mistakes – Bathsheba, mourning for the death of both her husband and son; the graves of both Uriah and the son born out of David's night with the dead man's wife.

You could be forgiven for thinking that it was against this husband and wife that David had sinned, but he has realised something profound: 'Against you, you only, have I sinned and done what is evil in your sight, so that you are proved right when you speak and justified when you judge' (Psalm 51:4).

He's right too; it was when he turned his back on God, when he stopped doing what was right in his anointed and appointed role that he started doing evil against other people. 'Surely I was sinful at birth, sinful from the time my mother conceived me' (Psalm 51:5). This is a controversial point, as some scholars have suggested that David was an illegitimate child, the product of his father Jesse's relationship outside of marriage, with another woman. It is suggested that these facts about his conception made David far more likely to sin sexually. I find that a hard line of argument to follow, leading on to the rocky ground of superstition and a denial of responsibility. What I do agree with, though, is that David probably had a weakness for the ladies, regardless of his birth. Perhaps his life was a constant battle between his urge for sexual adventure and his desire to serve his God. Let's face it, he wouldn't be alone in that, would he?

We all have particular areas of weakness, sins that we are more likely to turn towards than others. These may well be as a result of our childhood; if we were raised against a backdrop of an abusive and destructive relationship it stands to reason that our own approach to relationships might be slightly off-centre. If we are told every day that responsibility is a bad thing, that we need to look out for number one regardless of what others may say, then it wouldn't surprise many people if we turned out selfish and unwilling to commit to things and people. The solution? David has it right here: 'Surely you desire truth in the inner parts; you teach me wisdom in the inmost place' (Psalm 51:6).

That's it, we need wisdom. As the ultimate Creator, the all-seeing I am, God knows us like no one else ever could. We need his wisdom and his insight. Ask him why and where you might fall down. Ask him for help in readjusting some of your beliefs and values. Like David, ask for a total overhaul: 'Cleanse me with hyssop, and I shall be clean; wash me, and I shall be whiter than snow' (Psalm 51:7).

This is a key truth for us as Christians. Only Jesus' blood can wash us clean, only forgiveness that comes direct from the Father can wipe away our guilt. If we turn to him and genuinely ask for forgiveness, acknowledging what we have done wrong, then he will restore us, he will bring us back on home to the place where we . . .

> . . . hear joy and gladness; let the bones you have crushed rejoice. Hide your face from my sins and blot out all my iniquity. Create in me a pure heart, O God, and renew a steadfast spirit within me. Do not cast me from your presence or take your Holy Spirit from me. Restore to me the joy of your salvation and grant me a willing spirit, to sustain me.
>
> (Psalm 51:8–12)

One of the most obvious signs that we've messed up is that we lose the 'joy of our salvation'; things can become stale and dry as we drift further away from God (although when they do it doesn't automatically mean that we've sinned). The good news is that God can restore that joy, nothing is irredeemable.

It may be that you're going through a period where you're dealing with disappointment and doubt at the moment, not because your dreams have been wasted and not because your potential has been left stranded at the roadside. It may simply be that things are tough because you've messed up. Well, join the club. Get back up and run the race; make your apologies –

you may need someone to help you – and start again.
With God, there's always a second chance.

'If you look for truth, you may find comfort in the end: if you look for comfort, you will not get either comfort or truth.'

C.S. Lewis

'Heroes are not
the ones that never fail, but the ones that never give up.'

Ed Cole

6

When You're Just Not Sure

Thomas's Story

As a fresh-faced, wide-eyed and innocent new Christian, I was hungry for knowledge. Sitting in my room I worked my way through countless books on different aspects of faith – you know the sort of thing: *How to Annoy Satan in Three Easy Steps* and *Why God Makes Good Christians Wealthy Overnight*. These were all very nice and entertaining, but something about them didn't quite hit the spot, something wasn't quite right.

It all made sense as soon as I returned from my local Christian bookshop with an entirely new type of book under my arm. It was an autobiography of some perfectly dentured American pastor, and little did I know that it would change things for me big time. Within minutes of starting to read this wonderful tome, I was captivated; all those other books had been so impersonal but here was a real-life person I could look up to and place on a pedestal. With the turning of each page came stories of spiritual battles fought and won, of trials and disasters which Pastor X sailed through with flying colours, faith and perfect smile well and truly intact. Whatever the devil threw at him – illness, bankruptcy, bereavement or faulty air-conditioning in his hotel suite – he fought back with steroid faith and the sure knowledge that he was able to give Satan's butt a right royal kicking.

This was the start of something new for me, and over the following months I became fascinated by this kind of Christian autobiography. I must have read hundreds of examples of it, each one giving me a new hero to follow, a new pin-up flexing his spiritual muscles to be admired. At first they made me feel great about myself; if they could sail through life's difficulties, perhaps I could too. Peering into the future I wondered what mine might contain; sure, there would be tough times, but there I'd be, striding along its highway, full of faith. Who knows, perhaps I'd even get to write books about my own victories one day.

After almost a year of this stuff it all started to go wrong. I had come across some kind of spiritual obstacle (can't remember what, exactly, but it was probably something to do with wondering whether God actually liked me) and nothing seemed to make sense. According to the world of Pastor X and friends, there was no room for doubt in the Victorious Christian Life. Life was for living, and doing it right meant believing 100 per cent that God was on your side and that everything was going to be A-OK.

Unfortunately things didn't seem like they were going to work out all right, and I certainly didn't feel full of faith. There had been a miracle on every page of the famous Christian minister's books, nothing had seemed to phase him and life had been one big advert for how the Lord sorted his mates out with a nice life. After months of lapping it up, I realised a profound truth about these authors. There was no denying the fact that my life just wasn't like theirs. I wanted to kill them.

Now that I get to write books and look serious whenever I'm on stage at a meeting, I need to be honest about a few things. My life still isn't like that of Pastor X and all the other faith warriors. It seems that even more than ever I'm plagued by doubt and confusion, and there certainly isn't a miracle on every page. I've got a feeling that yours is probably a bit like mine too, with there being more mess-ups than miracles, more confusion than canonisation. Above all, I bet there's been plenty of one thing that always seemed to have been flushed away by Pastor X et al: doubt.

But how do we do this Christian thing, then? How do we make sure that what we have holds together when all around us things seem to be crashing down? How do we deal with it when we aren't sure if God cares or even whether he exists? Is it fair to preach that we should never doubt our God? Whatever the cause – whether it's bereavement, redundancy, the breakdown of a relationship or the realisation that what seemed to be a plan with God's seal of approval on it has turned out to be a dud – life is full of reasons for us to question and to doubt our beliefs.

My own doubts come in various forms. At times I lie in bed wondering whether God really exists. At times I lie in bed wondering whether I really exist. Then there are the occasions when I have no problem whatsoever believing that God exists; what I struggle with is the question of whether or not he is *good*. I mean, there's so much evil in the world, can he really overcome it all? There are even times when I wonder whether he cares at all. Sometimes we Christians can put another spin on it, agreeing that God does exist and that he is good and loving, but that he doesn't actually love me. Then there are the other times when we're off on a mission that we may feel has been inspired by God himself when in creep those nagging doubts into our minds. The possibilities for doubt are endless, and I don't believe there's a Christian out there who doesn't go through it from time to time.

This is where it all gets confusing; you see I'm convinced – by my own life and others – that it is possible to have faith in God as well as to doubt. But here are the big questions: Does the doubt undermine the faith? Does the fact that we question God cancel out our belief in him? Is doubt like a virus, systematically destroying us and sapping our strength?

Surprisingly, my answer is: 'Well, it depends.' It all depends on how you define faith. Let me explain –

you see, in my book, faith is more than an 'intellectual ascent to a set of propositions' (actually, I found that in somebody else's book, but I thought it sounded clever so I nicked it). It's not just about building up your knowledge of history and understanding of the Bible to a point where you can deliver a sixty-minute lecture on why Jesus existed. Faith is not about spewing facts or understanding words like 'eschatological' and 'God'. Don't get me wrong, though. I believe that it is important that we grapple with the facts and exercise our God-given intellect in these matters, but there's more to faith than that.

Faith is also more than a nice gooey feeling. Simply relying on the emotional highs that go with the rhythms of the Christian life is not enough. Becoming a Spirit junky, desperate for the next dose of Holy Ghost up the front at church will never breed real faith. But of course, ignoring the fact that Christianity works on an emotional as well as an intellectual level will surely lead to trouble further on down the road.

The solution is to look in the Bible, where you will find something interesting about the word 'faith'. In my opinion, the Scriptures paint a picture of faith being a verb – a doing word – rather than a static noun. We'll do some digging around in a bit, and throughout we will see that faith is far more something that you do, something to be practised and worked on rather than something that is merely acquired, like a jumper or a set of bath salts.

For what it's worth, my experience tells me that faith is the ability to keep on heading towards God, trusting in him, when we are surrounded by doubts. Some people say that faith is the opposite of doubt, that you cannot have faith and be in doubt at the same time. I don't agree; just remember the time when Peter and friends were out fishing one night and saw Jesus come towards them walking on the water. 'Come on, sunshine,' he said to Pete. 'Let's go for a stroll.' Peter duly climbs out of the boat and does a bit of the old no-sinking routine. All seems to be going well until Peter sees the wind and is reminded of the fact that by rights, he should be sinking fast. He begins to doubt and starts to sink, fast. Jesus wanders over, picks him up and delivers the line about 'you of little faith'.

This story at first glance can seem to have a pretty clear message on the subject of faith. Many have used it in the past to back up their claim that doubt is the opposite of faith. The truth, however, is far more exciting. Ask yourself, who had the faith? Was it Peter, the one who walked on the water, sank and then got rescued by Jesus, or was it the disciples sat in the boat with their tails between their legs, refusing to budge? I think it was Peter who got the pat on the back in this case; surely God wants us to have the faith to get out of the boat, to take that initial bold step to trust him. We should be like Peter who, when Jesus told him to come for a non-dip, asked, 'If that's you out there, tell me and I'll come.' The other disciples could have sat there muttering to themselves about how convinced they were that it was Jesus out there, or perhaps they might have been whooping and high-fiving each other, pumped up by how good they felt about the whole thing. Only Peter got out of the boat. He was the only one that *did*; the others simply *were*.

Like Peter, we too can often end up surrounded by doubts once we've taken a step of faith. But like Peter too, having taken that step towards him, we give Jesus the opportunity to come and pick us up. This leads us nicely up to the front door of an essential truth; faith is an adventure. What's more, I am convinced that instead of being the opposite of faith, doubt is the journey we take to come to faith.

The key to this side of the Christian life is keeping going with God despite the inevitable doubts and hiccups that colour our insecure moments. Right now as I write, in December 1999, I'm going through one of those insecure moments. Actually, 'insecure moment' doesn't quite do it justice; I think 'month of blind panic' would be more precise. You see, in precisely seven months, three weeks and four days, Soul Survivor will open the doors on its biggest event yet, just as this book gets published. The summer of 2000 will see us all hike up to Manchester for two week-long missions that aim to make a serious impact on a generation in and around the city. The Message 2000 is all about getting ordinary people to put their faith into practice by taking part in this massive mission, which needs almost 20,000 people to make it work. I firmly believe that the idea has come from God himself. I'm convinced he's into it, that he has said that he will honour and bless it.

81

Sitting here in my flat, staring out at the grey skies, I'm beginning to get a little worried. We have 104 people booked in for the first week and 43 for the second. Did I mention that we needed 20,000 to make it work? That's *19,853* left to go. Oh dear. Right now I wake up at 2 a.m., rigid with fear and cold with worry. Faced with the potential of losing hundreds of thousands of pounds I conjure up elaborate rescue plans. First I sell my flat, then I record a novelty single that goes straight in at number one. It uses the 'I feel like chicken tonight' melody and contains the following lyrics:

> I quite like bacon for tea
> Oinky oinky oinky oink
> I quite like lamb chops for lunch
> Baa baa baa baa baa baa.
> I quite like chocolate for afters . . .

I'm having trouble finding the noise that chocolate makes, but I'm pretty sure that the rest of it's a winner. With such a sure-fire hit as this up my sleeve, you may be surprised to hear that there are times when even 'Bacon for Tea' doesn't seem quite enough to banish worry and doubt from my mind. I'm left with feelings of doubt, and we are old friends. When our church decided to buy and refurbish a derelict warehouse, there were doubts about whether we could afford it. When we put on our first Soul Survivor festival there were doubts about whether anyone would come along. When I accepted the offer of running a youth group in my old church, there they were again, the doubts that asked whether I really could do it. But as well as the doubt, in each of these situations there was faith, made visible by the decision to keep on keeping on, no matter how wobbly or insecure I felt at the time.

I'm convinced that this thing called doubt is a gift from God, there to help us carry out quality-control checks on our faith. After all, faith was never meant to be a blind thing, something that was either on or off, present or absent. Faith is organic, needing to be fed, nurtured and tested. Without the opportunity to say, 'Yup, there are a few doubts around but I'm pressing on', what you're left with is untested and unproved. What use is that?

'Faith comes by hearing, and hearing by the word of God,' says the Bible. That means that our faith grows when we hear God's voice. It's easy enough to have a type of faith in all sorts of things which is little more than bravado or hype. The secret to picking yourself up off your knees in front of the empty tomb is having a tried and tested faith.

There's a character in the Bible who is spot on when it comes to any discussion of faith and doubt. No prizes for guessing that I'm talking about Thomas, AKA the Doubting Disciple. Where other disciples have been characterised as struggling with anger, fear or stupidity, history has recorded Thomas as the eternal pessimist. In John 14 we read about Jesus giving the people his 'in my father's house there are many rooms . . .' speech. He concludes with the most amazing promise anyone could ever ask for:

> I am going there to prepare a place for you. And if
> I go and prepare a place for you, I will come back
> and take you to be with me that you also may be
> where I am. You know the way to the place where
> I am going.
>
> (John 14:3–4)

If you ask me, it's pure dynamite. Apparently
Thomas, however, didn't agree.

> Thomas said to him, 'Lord, we don't know where
> you are going, so how can we know the way?'
> Jesus answered, 'I am the way and the truth and
> the life. No-one comes to the Father except
> through me.'
>
> (John 14:5–6)

It's bizarre; Jesus is giving them such an
encouragement yet you can almost hear Thomas
whining above the rest of them as they murmured
their appreciation. I think I would have been a lot
less gracious with him than Jesus. After all the time
they'd spent together, for Thomas to question such a
fundamental truth would certainly have earned him
a quick slap from me.

There's another story featuring Thomas which
crops up when Jesus heard that his friend Lazarus
had died:

After he had said this, he went on to tell them, 'Our friend Lazarus has fallen asleep; but I am going there to wake him up.'

His disciples replied, 'Lord, if he sleeps, he will get better.' Jesus had been speaking of his death, but his disciples thought he meant natural sleep.

So then he told them plainly, 'Lazarus is dead, and for your sake I am glad I was not there, so that you may believe. But let us go to him.'

Then Thomas (called Didymus) said to the rest of the disciples, 'Let us also go, that we may die with him.'

(John 11:11–16)

You can't get much bleaker than that. Dear old Tom, while Jesus was about to perform one of his most spectacular miracles, was preparing to die himself. Jesus had even prompted them that they were about to see something inspiring (when he said that he was glad that he 'was not there, so that [they] may believe'). Thomas couldn't have got it more wrong if he tried.

Finally we have the absolute classic as Jesus catches up with his followers after he was raised from the dead. Here Thomas takes full advantage of the opportunity and makes himself look like an utter fool.

Now Thomas (called Didymus), one of the Twelve, was not with the disciples when Jesus came. So the other disciples told him, 'We have seen the Lord!'

But he said to them, 'Unless I see the nail marks in his hands and put my finger where the nails were, and put my hand into his side, I will not believe it.'

A week later his disciples were in the house again, and Thomas was with them. Though the doors were locked, Jesus came and stood among them and said, 'Peace be with you!' Then he said to Thomas, 'Put your finger here; see my hands. Reach out your hand and put it into my side. Stop doubting and believe.'

Thomas said to him, 'My Lord and my God!'

Then Jesus told him, 'Because you have seen me, you have believed; blessed are those who have not seen and yet have believed.'

(John 20:24–9)

Thomas's cries of 'unless I see/touch/feel' almost seem like more than simple doubt, but a wilful stubbornness and a desire not to get caught out. Having made him wait a week, Jesus is kind to his dubious disciple, agreeing to his own conditions by encouraging Thomas to feel his wounds for himself. Suddenly Thomas the doubter speaks the words of faith: 'My Lord and my God!'

So what is the antidote to doubt? First up we shouldn't feel guilty that we question things. Everybody has doubts and there isn't a human among us who hasn't questioned their values and beliefs at some point. It's what separates us from the fish, and being able to question and press on in the face of opposition is a key step towards spiritual maturity. But more than that, the antidote for us is the same as it was for Peter and Thomas: to see Jesus. Jesus' words to Thomas were pure acceptance and encouragement – 'Come on home, son. It's OK to test me and have doubts. Feel these wounds and let them ease your doubts. Now follow me.'

For many of us, each time we have a crisis in our lives and everything seems to be going wrong we have the ideal opportunity to put our faith into action. That doesn't mean applying the fake tan and pearly white smile denying the existence of doubt. Instead it's time to admit the fears and take them back to the Lord. It's not failure, it's the opportunity to find a deeper understanding of God.

'However bleak
events may be, we cannot
interpret them as telling us that
God has ceased to be the loving,
all-powerful, fair and extravagant
heavenly Father that he is. Instead,
because he is like that, it means
our difficulties are in his
control and his purposes
for us are good.'

Peter Meadows

7

Beyond the Tomb
Paul's Story

I'm always amazed by the way that Jesus can turn lives around. No matter how far away or how determined we may have been to keep the distance between ourselves and our Creator, Jesus always holds the power to bring us back. You may be wondering where this power comes from; the answer is plain and simple, it comes from Jesus' death and resurrection. We've gone into it in much more detail in the first book of this series (*Walking with a Stranger*), but the fact that Jesus chose not only to die on the cross (taking the punishment that we deserve for all our sin) but then rose from the dead means that the message of Christianity is the most potent around. Because of Jesus we have a future in heaven and the power to overcome all obstacles. In his letter to the church in Rome, Paul suggested that if the resurrection was a hoax, then we Christians are to be pitied. You see, the resurrection is absolutely central to what we believe and without it our faith falls down.

With that kind of ammunition, it's not surprising that lives get turned around as people encounter Jesus one on one. There are hundreds of stories told by people who have had their own lives turned around, but if you ask me, there's one particular tale that stands head and shoulders above the rest: that man Paul. Way back in the days of the early church, throughout the years following Jesus' life on earth, Saul (as he was known back then) was a persecutor. Not only was he a pure grade, 100 per cent zealous Pharisee, but he was also a particularly nasty piece of work. He hated the sect of new Christians, and used his time productively by killing, persecuting or imprisoning as many of them as he could find. In fact, we read that when Stephen made it into the history books as the first Christian martyr, it was dear old Saul who was helpfully holding the coats of those who were stoning him to death. It was a tragedy for the early church (known as 'the people of the Way'), made even worse by the fact that Stephen was widely recognised as being a good man, full of faith and the Holy Spirit. He even echoed his Saviour, asking with his final words that his killers be forgiven.

This side of heaven we will probably never know what sort of impact this inspiring display of Christianity in action made on Saul, but by the time we reach Acts 9, we get to know him a whole lot better:

Meanwhile, Saul was still breathing out murderous threats against the Lord's disciples. He went to the high priest and asked him for letters to the synagogues in Damascus, so that if he found any there who belonged to the Way, whether men or women, he might take them as prisoners to Jerusalem. As he neared Damascus on his journey, suddenly a light from heaven flashed around him. He fell to the ground and heard a voice say to him, 'Saul, Saul, why do you persecute me?'

'Who are you, Lord?' Saul asked.

'I am Jesus, whom you are persecuting,' he replied. 'Now get up and go into the city, and you will be told what you must do.'

(Acts 9:1–6)

So, blinded and probably just a little confused, Saul makes his way to the city where he hooks up with a fine man by the name of Ananias. Within a few verses the story covers his conversion and we begin to glimpse the extent to which he has been transformed. Like many millions of others throughout time, Saul's transformation came when he met the risen Jesus. So extreme was this change that because of Paul's life, the rest of the Bible – in fact, the rest of Christianity – would never be quite the same again. Instead of knocking it down, he went on to build up the early church, making sure that it had strength and wisdom enough to see it through.

But it wasn't all plain sailing. If you thought that once he changed his name to Paul everything went smoothly, unfortunately you'd be wrong. For Paul, life was full of trials and tribulations; he was beaten, shipwrecked, arrested and put in jail. He was run out of town and faced death and opposition almost wherever he went. Yet he was fired up, fully committed to doing whatever it took to ensure the good progress of the message of Jesus Christ.

With such an impressive CV it's not surprising that he was responsible for depositing more than a few pearls of wisdom in his time. Of all his wise words, I reckon that some of the best can be found in his letter to the church at Philippi. It was no ordinary letter; not only is it stuffed full of reasons why his friends the Philippians ought to be rejoicing, but it was written while Paul was locked up in a Roman jail. He was permanently chained to a guard who was changed every six hours. Now there's an obvious reason why these guards were given six-hour shifts, but reading between the lines I'm convinced that it wasn't just the call of nature that had them bursting to unlock themselves and leave Paul's company. Paul, it would seem, saw the arrangement of chaining a guard to him as a perfect opportunity for evangelism, and he told his readers that . . .

> Now I want you to know, brothers, that what has happened to me has really served to advance the gospel. As a result, it has become clear throughout the whole palace guard and to everyone else that I am in chains for Christ. Because of my chains, most of the brothers in the Lord have been

encouraged to speak the word of God more courageously and fearlessly.

(Philippians 1:12–13)

He told his jailers all about his faith, and I bet for many of them it was one of the most taxing shifts going; I almost feel sorry for them. In the end there were believing Christians at the heart of Roman power – in the palace guard – all because of one Christian who just couldn't keep his gob shut.

This love of God-chat was so strong in Paul because he so profoundly realised that he had been saved. What is even more exciting is the fact that by many measures, he was doing pretty well in society's eyes before he met Jesus. As he puts it, his pedigree was near perfect:

If anyone else thinks he has reasons to put confidence in the flesh, I have more: circumcised on the eighth day, of the people of Israel, of the tribe of Benjamin, a Hebrew of Hebrews; in regard to the law, a Pharisee; as for zeal, persecuting the church; as for legalistic righteousness, faultless.

(Philippians 3:4b–6)

Not only was he a Jew, but he was a member of one of the better tribes. He was not only religious, he was professionally religious, and very good at it too. He was a top-notch social climber with a bright future in the persecution business. As he said, he had every reason to 'put confidence in the flesh', to rely on his own strengths, talents and abilities without turning elsewhere for assistance. He had it all, until he met Jesus:

> But whatever was to my profit I now consider loss for the sake of Christ. What is more, I consider everything a loss compared to the surpassing greatness of knowing Christ Jesus my Lord, for whose sake I have lost all things. I consider them rubbish, that I may gain Christ and be found in him, not having a righteousness of my own that comes from the law, but that which is through faith in Christ – the righteousness that comes from God and is by faith.
>
> (Philippians 3:7–9)

Bible translators tend to be fairly polite people, and so their choice of the word 'rubbish' here should not be taken too seriously. Instead, Paul's original letter in Greek would have contained something more like 'I consider all these things *dog dung* compared to knowing Christ'. He makes it clear that he found something far more worthwhile and exciting than the human talents and religious rituals that he was previously so reliant upon. Instead he shouts it from the rooftops that it was Jesus who made all the difference in his life. And like those attempts to get into the *Guinness Book of Records* for toppling dominoes, there's always a spectacular ending. Paul's argument leads up to this, one of my favourite verses in the Bible:

I want to know Christ and the power of his resurrection and the fellowship of sharing in his sufferings, becoming like him in his death, and so, somehow, to attain to the resurrection from the dead.

(Philippians 3:10)

Face facts; that verse rocks. Take the first bit, I mean, who wouldn't want to couple up with the Lord Almighty and share in some of his amazing power? But in the same way that God doesn't separate the twin elements of victory and pain in the cross, Paul keeps things in order. It can be all too easy for us Christians to get off on a happy 'n' holy trip, enjoying the good stuff of blessings and spiritual sunny days. As soon as the merest cloud appears on the horizon, as soon as there's a hint that things aren't going to be quite the picnic we had planned, we find it all too tempting to get in a big strop with God and refuse to keep moving on with him. But loving God truly means loving the tough stuff as well as the blessings. When Ananias was given his instructions about hosting Saul after his meeting with God along the road to Damascus, Ananias was understandably hesitant – I mean, wouldn't you be if faced with a similar proposition? Yet the Lord told Ananias that he was going to show Saul exactly how much he was going to suffer for him. Resurrection and suffering go hand in hand and, for our sake, Jesus went through the pain of the cross in order to reach the resurrection on the other side.

Being like Christ means being like Paul in the sense that sometimes we have to travel the harder path instead of enjoying the chauffeured limo. I believe suffering falls into two categories. First, there's the type of suffering that is dictated by circumstance – the illness, the poverty and the tragedy. Second, there's the type that we choose – the decision not to follow our own wills all the time but to sacrifice for the will of God. Like a parent getting up to answer the cries of a baby at night, or a lover clearing up after someone has been ill, this type of sacrifice sends a message loud and clear about how love is twinned with sacrifice.

I'm certainly not saying that if faced with a choice between a pleasurable and an unpleasant situation that it would be God's will that we automatically opt for the worst. We're not supposed to be miserable gits in hair shirts, but for all of us, surely it makes sense that if we really are following the God who laid down his life for us, then our lives will show reflections of that same spirit. There must be some situations when God's will and our will are in opposition and we end up choosing to go for his. Even Jesus in the Garden of Gethsemane went through this one. 'May this cup pass from me,' he pleaded with his father. The agony of the cross was just hours away, yet he followed on by saying, 'Not my will but yours be done.' That's the suffering that comes from obediently following.

And so we end up once again with Mary Magdalene, weeping before the empty tomb. The central message of Christianity comes in the death and the resurrection of Jesus Christ. He actually came in order to die. A man on a mission, he came to face death – the ultimate enemy of us all. He came to fight it and to conquer it, to announce a victory that is on offer to us all. Because Jesus died we don't need to weep before the tomb; it's empty and Jesus is long gone. He has risen, leaving the tomb and returning in glorious victory back to heaven. We don't need to mourn; the resurrection gives us hope. When life is tough like it was for Job or Joseph, when we have doubts like Thomas, mess up like David or Samson, in the end there's hope for us precisely because there's no one in the tomb. Because he rose our lives *can* change, they *can* be different. That's the hope which is available to us all, and that's what we will be going on to look at in the last of these four little books; the great hope of life after death.

'Never give in, never give in,
never, never, never — in nothing,
great or small, large or petty —
never give in except to convictions
of honour and good sense.'

Winston Churchill